AF601345

ARTIFICIAL AROMAS

A COFFEE TABLE BOOK ABOUT COFFEE BY AI

JERLYN X AI

Jerlyn Thomas

http://www.designlady.com

ISBN: 978-1-7361010-5-6

To all the coffee lovers worldwide, who wake up each day to the aroma of freshly brewed coffee, and to the farmers, roasters, baristas, and enthusiasts who make the coffee industry possible. This book is dedicated to your unwavering passion and love for the beautiful coffee beverage.

CONTENTS

68 V. HEALTH BENEFITS & CONTROVERSIES

It's important to note that coffee consumption's health benefits and risks can vary depending on individual factors such as age, genetics, and lifestyle. For example, pregnant women are advised to limit their caffeine intake due to potential risks to the developing fetus. It's always best to consult with a healthcare professional about whether coffee consumption is safe for you and how much is appropriate for your individual needs. In addition to its potential health benefits, coffee is also a source of pleasure and enjoyment for many people. Whether enjoyed alone or in the company of others, coffee can provide a sense of comfort and familiarity, especially during stressful or challenging times.

80 VI. THE FUTURE OF COFFEE

The coffee industry is constantly evolving, and the future of coffee looks promising. Sustainability and social responsibility will continue to be significant in coffee production, with consumers increasingly demanding ethically sourced and sustainable coffee. Coffee companies will likely continue implementing fair labor practices, reducing their carbon footprint, and supporting small-scale farmers. Technology is also crucial in the coffee industry, with advancements in roasting and brewing techniques allowing for greater precision and consistency in coffee preparation. Specialty coffee, which emphasizes high-quality beans and meticulous preparation, will continue to grow in popularity, leading to the development of new brewing methods that produce complex and nuanced cups of coffee.

96 VII. SAVORING THE LAST DROP

Let's celebrate the enduring love for coffee and its continued significance. As coffee lovers, we are responsible for appreciating the beauty and complexity of this great beverage while supporting sustainable and ethical practices that benefit coffee farmers, communities, and the planet. We'll end with a call to action - to appreciate coffee's beauty and complexity, support sustainable and ethical practices in the coffee industry, and share our love for coffee with others.

OPENING BLEND

Coffee is not just a drink, it's a journey through time and culture.

Coffee is more than just a beverage. It's a cultural touchstone that has brought people together across the globe for centuries. From its origins in Ethiopia, coffee has traveled the world, becoming essential to many cultures and traditions. But the story of coffee is more than just a history lesson. It's a journey through evolved flavors, aromas, and brewing methods. In this coffee table book, we'll explore the fascinating world of coffee, from its origins to its modern-day status as one of the world's most beloved beverages.

We'll dive deep into the origins of coffee, the different types of coffee beans, and the growing regions that produce some of the world's most famous coffees. We'll also explore the various brewing methods, from traditional pour-over to modern-day espresso machines, and the techniques and tools needed to make a great cup of coffee.

But coffee is more than just a drink. It has inspired art, literature, and music and has served as a meeting place for artists, intellectuals, and revolutionaries throughout history. In this book, we'll also explore coffee's cultural and social significance, from the cafes of Paris to the coffeehouses of Istanbul.

Throughout the book, we'll showcase stunning illustrations and images that capture the beauty and complexity of coffee. Whether you're a coffee lover or just interested in this beloved beverage's history and culture, this book will surely delight and inspire you. So sit back, pour yourself a cup of your favorite brew, and join us on a journey through the world of coffee. And when you're finished, be sure to share this book with your friends and family so they can experience the joy of coffee too.

Images that evoke the ancient history of coffee in Ethiopia, using warm colors and earthy tones to set the scene

Different types of coffee beans, using close-up shots and strong contrast to showcase their distinct colors and textures

Image reference + A model wearing a stunning dress with a coffee - bean motif, flowing hair

3D image on white Coffee shops and cafes around the world, with a collage of artistic coffee cups from different locations.

A BRIEF HISTORY OF COFFEE

A man is by his goats, asante art

Coffee has become integral to many daily routines, but its origins are shrouded in mystery and legend. The story of coffee begins in Ethiopia, where coffee trees are believed to have grown wild for thousands of years.

According to one popular myth, a goat herder named Kaldi discovered coffee's energizing properties after noticing his goats became particularly lively after eating the berries of a particular tree. From its humble beginnings in Ethiopia, coffee spread throughout the Arabian Peninsula and beyond, becoming a global phenomenon for centuries. Over time, coffee has played an essential role in shaping cultures and economies and has even been the subject of political and social controversies. Today, coffee is the second most traded commodity in the world and continues to be beloved beverage millions enjoy.

A simple yet striking image that showcases the global reach of coffee, using a minimalist style and strong typography to convey the importance of coffee in our daily lives

Coffee in art, featuring a selection of famous paintings that showcase coffee - drinking scenes

Coffee in art, featuring a selection of famous paintings that showcase coffee - drinking scenes

IMPORTANCE OF COFFEE IN CULTURES AROUND THE WORLD

Diorama against white background
Illustration of a bustling Italian cafe
with people sipping espresso and chatting
at outdoor tables

Coffee has played a significant role in shaping cultures around the world. From its origins in Ethiopia, coffee has traveled the globe, becoming essential to many cultures and traditions. In some places, coffee is more than just a beverage; it is a social and cultural institution that brings people together.

In Turkey, for example, coffee is often served as part of a traditional ceremony where guests are welcomed, and hospitality is shared. In Italy, coffee is a daily ritual enjoyed in cafes and bars nationwide. In many Latin American countries, coffee is a vital part of the economy and a source of national pride. The importance of coffee is not limited to drinking it either; coffee has also inspired art, literature, and music. Coffeehouses have served as meeting places for artists, intellectuals, and revolutionaries throughout history. In short, coffee is more than just a drink; it is a cultural touchstone that has brought people together across the globe.

Coffee cocktails and mocktails, with a mixologist shaking a coffee - based drink in a bar

Watercolor of a selection of vibrant fruits
and nuts arranged around a cup of coffee

Coffee and sustainability, with a collage of photos that depict eco - friendly coffee - growing practices

ROOTS OF THE ROAST

Gain a newfound appreciation for this beloved beverage's rich and complex story.

Through vivid descriptions and stunning imagery, we'll paint a vivid picture of the intricate web of factors that produce a great cup of coffee, from the soil and climate to the harvesting and processing techniques. By the end of this section, you'll have a newfound appreciation for this beloved beverage's rich history and diverse origins.

Illustration of a group of people gathered around a coffee pot or machine, enjoying a cup of coffee while chatting and socializing

Coffee's origin story is as intriguing as mysterious, steeped in myth and legend. Although the exact origins of coffee remain a matter of debate, there is no doubt that it has come a long way from its humble beginnings in Ethiopia. Today, coffee is a globally traded commodity, cultivated in different regions worldwide, each with its unique flavor profile and growing conditions that make it distinct.

In this section, we'll embark on a journey of discovery through the history of coffee, tracing its roots to its earliest days in Ethiopia, exploring the different types of coffee beans, and taking a closer look at the various growing regions that produce some of the world's most beloved coffees. We'll delve into the cultural significance of coffee in different societies and how it has evolved over the centuries.

From the wild coffee forests of Ethiopia to the sprawling coffee plantations of South America, let's explore the fascinating and complex world of coffee origins. Let's look at how coffee cultivation has shaped the lives of countless farmers and communities worldwide and how it continues to be a vital source of income for many people.

Crafted from volumetric felt and colorful 3D paper quilling of different types of coffee beans

A coffee bean in extreme close - up, with its rich texture and complex pattern taking center stage.

The history of coffee, featuring an antique coffee grinder and an old map of coffee - growing regions

ORIGIN OF COFFEE BEANS

Acrylic painting of Coffea plant

Coffee beans come from the fruit of the Coffea plant, which grows in tropical regions around the world. According to legend, the discovery of coffee's energizing properties dates back to ancient Ethiopia, where a goat herder named Kaldi noticed that his goats became particularly lively after eating the berries of a specific tree. Over time, coffee spread throughout the Arabian Peninsula and beyond, becoming a global phenomenon enjoyed for centuries. Let's explore the history and evolution of coffee beans and how they are harvested and processed.

Two primary methods for harvesting coffee are selective picking and strip picking. Selective picking involves harvesting only the ripest cherries by hand, a labor-intensive and time-consuming process that results in a higher-quality product. Using a machine, strip picking involves stripping all the cherries off the branch, regardless of ripeness.

After the coffee cherries are harvested, they undergo a processing stage to remove the outer layers and reveal the coffee beans. There are three main processing methods: the natural method, the washed method, and the honey method.

In the natural method, the coffee cherries are dried whole with the fruit still attached. This process takes longer, resulting in a sweeter and fruitier flavor profile. In the washed method, the outer layers of the coffee cherries are removed before the beans are washed and fermented. This method results in a cleaner and brighter flavor profile. The honey method is a hybrid of the natural and washed methods, where some of the fruit is removed, but some are left to dry on the beans, resulting in a unique flavor profile.

After the beans are processed, they are sorted and graded based on size, shape, and defects. The highest quality beans are usually sold to specialty coffee roasters, while lower quality beans may be used in commercial blends or instant coffee.

Overall, the harvesting and processing techniques used can significantly impact the coffee's final flavor profile.

A coffee tree with its leaves and berries, symbolizing the origin of coffee beans and how it all started with a goat herder in Ethiopia.

Coffee cherries being selectively picked by hand and strip-picked by a machine, highlighting the two primary methods for harvesting coffee

TYPES OF COFFEE BEANS

Digital knolling of Arabica and Robusta beans

There are two main types of coffee beans: Arabica and Robusta. Within these two types of beans are hundreds of different varieties, each with its unique flavor profile. Arabica beans are generally considered to be of higher quality and are grown in higher elevations, while Robusta beans are hardier and can be grown in lower elevations. In this chapter, we'll explore the differences between Arabica and Robusta beans and the various varieties of each.

Arabica and Robusta are the two most commonly cultivated coffee species, each with a distinct flavor profile, growing conditions, and harvesting and processing techniques.

Arabica coffee is known for its delicate and nuanced flavors, with fruit, chocolate, and nuts notes. It's typically grown at higher altitudes, where cooler temperatures and lower oxygen levels create an ideal growing environment. Arabica coffee plants are susceptible to pests and diseases, and their cultivation requires careful attention to soil conditions, watering, and pruning.

Robusta coffee, on the other hand, is known for its bold, earthy flavor and high caffeine content. It's typically grown at lower altitudes and in warmer climates, where it's less susceptible to pests and diseases. Robusta coffee plants are hardier and more resilient than Arabica plants, but they also require less attention to detail during cultivation.

Within each species, different varieties of coffee have been developed over the years. For example, some of the most famous Arabica varieties include Typica, Bourbon, and Caturra, each with unique flavor profiles and growing conditions. Similarly, some of the most popular Robusta varieties include Robusta Congo, Robusta Java, and Robusta Uganda.

The different varieties of coffee are often selected for their flavor, disease resistance, and adaptability to specific growing conditions. Growers often experiment with different types and cultivation techniques to find the best combination for their climate and soil conditions. Overall, the differences between Arabica and Robusta beans and their various varieties play a significant role in determining the final flavor and quality of the coffee we enjoy.

A coffee farm with different varieties of Arabica and Robusta coffee plants growing side by side, showcasing the variations in the shape, size, and color of the coffee cherries

A coffee roaster, with different batches of Arabica and Robusta beans roasting in separate machines, showcasing the differences in the roasting process and the resulting flavor profiles of the two types of coffee

GROWING REGIONS AND THEIR UNIQUE CHARACTERISTICS

Image reference + an older man with a hat standing in a valley with mountains and lush vegetation

Coffee is grown in regions around the world, from Latin America to Africa to Asia. Each region has unique growing conditions, which can impact the flavor of the coffee beans. This chapter will explore some of the world's most famous coffee-growing areas, including Brazil, Colombia, Ethiopia, and Indonesia. We'll also look at the unique characteristics of each region, such as soil type, altitude, and climate, and how these factors can impact the flavor of the coffee beans.

Brazil is the largest coffee producer globally, accounting for roughly 40% of the world's coffee. The country's coffee is typically low-acidic and has a mild flavor due to the large-scale production of the Arabica variety. Brazil's coffee is grown at low altitudes, with a tropical climate and fertile soil, making it perfect for growing coffee beans.

Colombia is another significant player in the coffee industry, mainly producing Arabica beans. Colombian coffee is known for its mild, well-balanced flavor and a hint of caramel or chocolate. The country's coffee is grown at high altitudes, with rich volcanic soil and a cool climate that provides the perfect conditions for growing coffee beans.

Ethiopia is the birthplace of coffee, and it's no surprise that it produces some of the world's best coffee. Ethiopian coffee is typically grown at high altitudes, and the country's diverse geography and climate provide a range of flavor profiles. The coffee is known for its floral and fruity notes, with some varieties having hints of wine or chocolate.

Indonesia is a unique coffee-growing region, producing both Arabica and Robusta beans. The country's coffee is grown in the fertile volcanic soil of the islands, with a tropical climate and high humidity. Indonesian coffee has a unique flavor profile, with earthy and spicy notes and a full body.

The unique characteristics of each region, such as soil type, altitude, and climate, impact the flavor of the coffee beans. For example, high-altitude coffee tends to have a more complex flavor profile due to the slower ripening of the beans. At the same time, the soil's composition can affect the coffee's acidity and body. The climate also plays a crucial role, as rainfall, temperature, and humidity can all affect the coffee beans' quality.

In conclusion, the world's most famous coffee-growing regions have unique flavor profiles shaped by their growing conditions. From the mild, low-acidic coffee of Brazil to the complex flavor profile of Ethiopian coffee, each region has something unique to offer the coffee connoisseur.

A traditional Ethiopian coffee ceremony, with colorful coffee cups and a clay coffee pot, highlighting the country's cultural significance and its contribution to the coffee industry

A coffee processing plant in Indonesia, with workers sorting and packaging the beans against the backdrop of a volcanic landscape, emphasizing the unique growing conditions of the region.

COFFEE ROASTING AND BREWING

These final stages of coffee preparation are where the coffee beans undergo a remarkable transformation

Roasting and brewing are the crucial last steps in the fascinating journey of coffee beans. Roasting and brewing, in particular, are essential to unlocking the rich flavors and aroma hidden within these beans. After the coffee cherries are carefully harvested, sorted, and processed, they are transformed into the flavorful and aromatic coffee beans we know and love.

Roasting, in particular, is a skillful art form that requires expertise, experience, and precision. The roasting process involves heating the green coffee beans to a specific temperature for a precise duration to bring out the desired flavor profile. Roasting methods vary widely, from traditional drum roasting to modern air roasting, each with unique flavor outcomes. The roasting level can also significantly impact the final taste, aroma, and body of the coffee, from light roasts that retain the natural flavors and acidity of the beans to dark roasts that develop rich, smoky, and bold flavors.

Brewing is the next step in the process, where coffee enthusiasts extract the flavor, aroma, and body from the roasted coffee beans. Factors such as water temperature, coffee-to-water ratio, and brewing time can affect the coffee's flavor, body, and acidity. Different brewing methods, from classic drip coffee to trendy pour-over, can dramatically influence the final taste and aroma of the coffee.

Specialty coffee drinks, such as lattes, cappuccinos, and espressos, add another layer of complexity to the coffee roasting and brewing process. These drinks are often made using specific brewing techniques and specialty coffee blends, resulting in unique and complex flavors that are highly sought after by coffee connoisseurs.

Overall, the roasting and brewing process is an essential aspect of the coffee industry, where attention to detail, expertise, and passion are necessary to produce high-quality coffee. Understanding the ins and outs of coffee roasting and brewing can help you appreciate the effort and artistry of making a delicious cup of coffee.

A barista preparing a pour-over coffee with a digital timer displaying the brewing time

A latte art competition, with baristas creating intricate designs on the surface of the coffee using steamed milk

A coffee laboratory, with scientists analyzing the chemical composition of coffee to better understand its flavor and aroma profiles

Image reference + a skilled coffee roaster standing beside a roasting machine, carefully monitoring the beans as they roast, with wisps of aromatic smoke rising in the background

Image Reference + a close-up shot of a barista pouring hot water over a coffee filter in a pour-over brewing method, capturing the mesmerizing flow of water through the grounds

THE ROASTING PROCESS

A coffee roasting drum with beans turning inside while being roasted, surrounded by flames and smoke

Roasting and brewing are the crucial last steps in the fascinating journey of coffee beans. Roasting and brewing, in particular, are essential to unlocking the rich flavors and aroma hidden within these beans. After the coffee cherries are carefully harvested, sorted, and processed, they are transformed into the flavorful and aromatic coffee beans we know and love.

Roasting, in particular, is a skillful art form that requires expertise, experience, and precision. The roasting process involves heating the green coffee beans to a specific temperature for a precise duration to bring out the desired flavor profile. Roasting methods vary widely, from traditional drum roasting to modern air roasting, each with unique flavor outcomes. The roasting level can also significantly impact the final taste, aroma, and body of the coffee, from light roasts that retain the natural flavors and acidity of the beans to dark roasts that develop rich, smoky, and bold flavors.

Brewing is the next step in the process, where coffee enthusiasts extract the flavor, aroma, and body from the roasted coffee beans. Factors such as water temperature, coffee-to-water ratio, and brewing time can affect the coffee's flavor, body, and acidity. Different brewing methods, from classic drip coffee to trendy pour-over, can dramatically influence the final taste and aroma of the coffee.

Specialty coffee drinks, such as lattes, cappuccinos, and espressos, add another layer of complexity to the coffee roasting and brewing process. These drinks are often made using specific brewing techniques and specialty coffee blends, resulting in unique and complex flavors that are highly sought after by coffee connoisseurs.

Overall, the roasting and brewing process is an essential aspect of the coffee industry, where attention to detail, expertise, and passion are necessary to produce high-quality coffee. Understanding the ins and outs of coffee roasting and brewing can help you appreciate the effort and artistry of making a delicious cup of coffee.

The Roasting Process

The roasting process can take anywhere from 5 to 20 minutes, depending on the desired roast level. The roasting process releases volatile compounds that contribute to the coffee's aroma and flavor. The roasting process can also affect the coffee's acidity, body, and bitterness. The roasting process is a complex and delicate process that requires skill and experience.

The Different Roast Levels

The different roast levels are classified as follows:

- Light roast: Light roasts have a short roasting time and retain the natural flavors and acidity of the beans. Light roasts are often described as having a bright, fruity, or floral aroma and flavor.
- Medium roast: Medium roasts have a medium roasting time and develop a more complex flavor profile than light roasts. Medium roasts are often described as having a smooth, balanced flavor.
- Dark roast: Dark roasts have a long roasting time and develop a rich, smoky, and bold flavor. Dark roasts are often described as having a full-bodied flavor.
-

The Different Roasting Methods

There are three main roasting methods:

- Drum roasting: Drum roasting is the most common roasting method. In drum roasting, the green coffee beans are roasted in a rotating drum that is heated from below.
- Fluid bed roasting: Fluid bed roasting is a more recent roasting method. In fluid bed roasting, the green coffee beans are roasted in a stream of hot air.
- Infrared roasting: Infrared roasting is a newer roasting method that uses infrared radiation to heat the green coffee beans.
- The Factors That Affect the Flavor of Roasted Coffee

The following factors can affect the flavor of roasted coffee:

- Roast level: The roast level is the most important factor that affects the flavor of roasted coffee. Light roasts have a bright, fruity, or floral aroma and flavor, while dark roasts have a rich, smoky, and bold flavor.
- Origin: The origin of the beans also affects the flavor of roasted coffee. Beans grown in different regions have different terroir, which can affect the flavor of the coffee.
- Altitude: The altitude at which the beans were grown also affects the flavor of roasted coffee. Beans grown at higher altitudes tend to have a more acidic and complex flavor profile.

The Importance of Quality Control in the Roasting Process

Quality control is important in the roasting process to ensure that the coffee is roasted to the desired level and that the flavor is consistent. Quality control measures include monitoring the temperature, time, and airflow during the roasting process.

Illustration of different roast levels side by side, ranging from light to dark, demonstrating the visual differences and highlighting how the roast level can affect the flavor and appearance of the coffee beans

Illustration of different roast levels side by side, ranging from light to dark, demonstrating the visual differences and highlighting how the roast level can affect the flavor and appearance of the coffee beans

DIFFERENT BREWING METHODS

An oil painting of an espresso machine with a shot of espresso being poured into a demitasse cup, with the rich, creamy crema visible on top

Brewing coffee is a process of extracting the flavor and aroma from coffee beans using hot water. The resulting beverage is known as coffee. Coffee is one of the most popular beverages in the world, and it is enjoyed by people of all ages.

There are many different ways to brew coffee, but the most common methods are drip brewing, French press brewing, pour-over brewing, and espresso brewing. Each method has its own unique characteristics, and the resulting coffee will vary depending on the method used.

Drip Brewing

Drip brewing is the most common method of brewing coffee. It is a simple and easy method that produces a consistent cup of coffee. In drip brewing, hot water is poured over coffee grounds in a filter, and the brewed coffee drips into a carafe below.

French Press Brewing

French press brewing is a more flavorful method of brewing coffee. It involves steeping coarse coffee grounds in hot water and pressing the plunger to separate the coffee from the grounds. French press coffee is known for its rich, full-bodied flavor.

Pour-Over Brewing

Pour-over brewing is a versatile method of brewing coffee. It can be used to brew a variety of coffees, and it is known for its clean, bright flavor. In pour-over brewing, hot water is poured over coffee grounds in a filter, allowing the coffee to drip into a carafe.

Espresso Brewing

Espresso brewing is a quick and efficient method of brewing coffee. It is used to make espresso, which is a strong, concentrated coffee. In espresso brewing, hot water is forced through tightly packed, finely ground coffee in an espresso machine. The resulting shot is rich, creamy, and full-bodied, with a layer of crema on top.

Brewing Method	*Pros*	*Cons*
Drip coffee	Simple to use, consistent cup of coffee	Weak and watery
French press	Richer body and more complex flavor	Oily and bitter if grounds are not ground coarsely enough
Pour-over	Versatile, clean, bright flavor	Time-consuming, requires a steady hand
Espresso	Strong, concentrated flavor	Bitter if beans are not fresh or espresso is not made correctly

How to Brew the Perfect Cup of Coffee

To brew the perfect cup of coffee, there are a few key things to keep in mind. First, use fresh, high-quality coffee beans. Second, grind the coffee beans to the correct coarseness. Third, use filtered water. Fourth, heat the water to the correct temperature. Fifth, time the brewing process correctly. Finally, enjoy!

Here are some additional tips for brewing the perfect cup of coffee:

Brewing Temperature

The brewing temperature is important for extracting the flavor and aroma from the coffee grounds. The ideal brewing temperature is between 195 and 205 degrees Fahrenheit. If the water is too hot, it will extract bitter flavors from the coffee grounds. If the water is too cold, it will not extract enough flavor from the coffee grounds.

Brewing Time

The brewing time is also important for extracting the flavor and aroma from the coffee grounds. The ideal brewing time is between 4 and 5 minutes. If the coffee is brewed for too long, it will become bitter. If the coffee is brewed for too short of a time, it will be weak.

Grind Size

The grind size is also important for brewing coffee. The grind size affects the rate at which the coffee is extracted. A finer grind will extract the coffee more quickly, while a coarser grind will extract the coffee more slowly. The ideal grind size for drip coffee is medium-coarse. The ideal grind size for French press coffee is coarse. The ideal grind size for pour-over coffee is medium-fine.

Water Quality

The water quality is also important for brewing coffee. The ideal water for brewing coffee is filtered water. Filtered water will remove impurities from the water that can affect the flavor of the coffee.

Storage

Coffee beans should be stored in an airtight container in a cool, dark place. Coffee beans should be used within 2 weeks of roasting.
Enjoy!

The most important thing is to enjoy your coffee! Experiment with different brewing methods and ratios to find the perfect cup of coffee for you.

A French press brewing process, featuring a French press filled with coffee grounds and hot water, with the plunger being pressed down to separate the brewed coffee

A pastel illustration a pour-over brewing method, with a barista pouring hot water over coffee grounds in a filter, highlighting the precision and skill required for this brewing technique

SPECIALTY COFFEE DRINKS

A cold brew, with ice cubes and a slice of lemon in a tall glass, on a black background with some coffee beans and a pouring kettle

Coffee is more than just a hot beverage. It's also the foundation for specialty coffee drinks, from lattes to cappuccinos to cold brew. In this chapter, we'll explore the history and evolution of some of the most popular specialty coffee drinks, including the latte, the cappuccino, the mocha, and the cold brew. We'll also look at the different ingredients and techniques used to create these drinks and how to make them at home.

Specialty coffee drinks have come a long way since the simple cup of coffee. These drinks have become a favorite of many coffee lovers worldwide. From the creamy and frothy lattes to the decadent mochas, there's no shortage of variety in the world of specialty coffee drinks.

One of the most popular specialty coffee drinks is the latte. The origin of the latte can be traced back to Italy in the 1950s. A latte is typically made with steamed milk and espresso. The steamed milk is poured into the espresso, creating a creamy and frothy layer. Lattes can be made with various flavors, including vanilla, caramel, and hazelnut. To make a latte at home, start by brewing a strong espresso shot, then steam milk to create a velvety texture and pour it over the espresso.

Another beloved specialty coffee drink is the cappuccino. The cappuccino also originated in Italy and is made using equal parts espresso, steamed, and frothed milk. The milk is heated to create a creamy texture, and the espresso is poured over it. The frothed milk is added on top of the espresso, creating a foam layer. To make a cappuccino at home, brew a strong espresso shot, steam milk to create a creamy texture, then pour the frothed milk on top.

Mocha, also known as a mochaccino, is a decadent specialty coffee drink that combines espresso, chocolate syrup, and steamed milk. The drink is typically topped with whipped cream and chocolate shavings. To make a mocha at home, start by brewing a strong espresso shot, then add chocolate syrup to the espresso. Steam milk to create a velvety texture and pour it over the espresso and chocolate mixture. Finally, add whipped cream and chocolate shavings on top.

Cold brew is another popular specialty coffee drink that has gained popularity in recent years. Cold brew is made by steeping coffee grounds in cold water for several hours, resulting in a smooth and less acidic flavor. The cold brew can be served over ice and mixed with various flavors, including vanilla, caramel, and hazelnut. Add coffee grounds to cold water and steep for 12-24 hours to make cold brew at home. Strain the mixture and serve over ice.

In conclusion, the history and evolution of specialty coffee drinks have been fascinating, with new variations emerging every year. Whether you prefer a classic latte or a trendy cold brew, there's a specialty coffee drink to suit every taste. With some knowledge and creativity, anyone can make a delicious specialty coffee drink at home.

The Latte

The latte is a coffee drink made with espresso and steamed milk. The ratio of espresso to steamed milk is typically 1:3. Lattes can be made with any type of milk, but whole milk is the most common. Lattes can also be flavored with syrups, such as vanilla, caramel, or hazelnut.

The Cappuccino

The cappuccino is a coffee drink made with espresso, steamed milk, and foamed milk. The ratio of espresso to steamed milk to foamed milk is typically 1:1:1. Cappuccinos are typically topped with a dusting of cocoa powder.

The Mocha

The mocha is a coffee drink made with espresso, chocolate syrup, and steamed milk. The ratio of espresso to chocolate syrup to steamed milk is typically 1:1:2. Mochas are typically topped with whipped cream and chocolate shavings.

The Cold Brew

Cold brew is a coffee drink made by steeping coffee grounds in cold water for several hours. The resulting coffee is smooth and less acidic than coffee made with hot water. Cold brew can be served over ice or blended with milk and other ingredients to make a variety of coffee drinks.

3d image render of a rich and indulgent mocha, with whipped cream and chocolate shavings on top, highlighting the decadence of this specialty coffee drink on white background

Illustration a variety of specialty coffee drinks side by side, including a latte, cappuccino, mocha, and cold brew, symbolizing the diverse range of options available in the world of specialty coffee

COFFEE CULTURE

Coffee is cultural fabric, connecting people across borders, generations, and cultures.

Coffee culture has become a way of life for millions worldwide, reflecting their unique traditions and values. From the social aspect of gathering with friends and loved ones to the ritualistic preparation of the perfect cup, coffee culture reflects the diverse customs and cultures of the world. Whether it's the small, independent coffee shops in the back alleys of Istanbul or the sleek, modern cafes in Tokyo, coffee culture is a universal language that brings people together.

The role of coffee shops in communities has also evolved over time, from places of intellectual discussion and political dissent to cozy meeting places for friends and family. Coffee shops have become a cultural hub for many, where people can come together, relax, and connect with each other. These spaces provide a sense of community and belonging, creating a sense of home for people in unfamiliar places.

The aroma, taste, and texture of coffee have become the muse for countless works of art, literature, and music, from the Impressionist paintings of Manet and Degas to the writings of Proust and Hemingway. Coffee has also inspired artists, writers, and musicians, fueling their creativity and imagination. The rhythm and melody of coffeehouse jazz and the upbeat energy of indie rock are just a few examples of how coffee culture has influenced music over the years.

No matter how it is enjoyed, coffee has become an integral part of the world's cultural fabric, connecting people across borders, generations, and cultures. Whether it's a simple cup of black coffee or an elaborate specialty drink, the art, science, and community surrounding this beloved beverage, continue to inspire and enrich our lives.

A heart shaped coffee cup has heart shaped hearts drawn in the top, in the style of digital airbrushing

A heart shaped coffee cup has heart shaped hearts drawn in the top, in the style of digital airbrushing

An illustration of a musician performing in a coffeehouse, surrounded by patrons sipping coffee and listening to the soulful melody of his guitar. The image captures the warmth and intimacy of coffeehouse music

The History of Coffee Culture

Coffee culture has a long and rich history that dates back to the 15th century. The first coffeehouses were opened in the Middle East, and they quickly became popular gathering places for people of all walks of life. Coffeehouses were places where people could discuss politics, philosophy, and religion, and they played an important role in the development of intellectual thought.

Coffee culture spread to Europe in the 17th century, and it quickly became popular there as well. Coffeehouses became popular meeting places for artists, writers, and intellectuals, and they played an important role in the development of the Enlightenment.

In the 18th century, coffee culture spread to the Americas, and it quickly became popular there as well. Coffeehouses became popular meeting places for people of all walks of life, and they played an important role in the development of American culture.

Today, coffee culture is enjoyed by people all over the world. Coffeehouses are popular gathering places for people of all ages, and they offer a variety of coffee drinks and food items. Coffee culture is a vibrant and dynamic part of the world's cultural fabric, and it continues to evolve and grow.

The Role of Coffee in Art and Literature

Coffee has been a muse for artists and writers for centuries. The aroma, taste, and texture of coffee have inspired countless works of art, literature, and music.

Some of the most famous paintings and sculptures that depict coffee include:

- "The Turkish Coffee House" by Jean-Antoine Watteau (1717)
- "The Coffee House" by Jan Steen (1660)
- "The Coffee Pot" by Jean-Siméon Chardin (1723)
- "The Cup of Coffee" by Francesco Hayez (1844)

Some of the most famous works of literature that mention coffee include:

- "The Coffee House" by Charles Dickens (1850)
- "The Coffee House Politician" by William Makepeace Thackeray (1847)
- "The Coffee Break" by James Joyce (1922)
- "The Coffee Shop" by John Updike (1981)

Some of the most famous songs that mention coffee include:

- "Coffee Song" by Simon & Garfunkel (1966)
- "Coffee Break" by Simon & Garfunkel (1966)
- "I'm Your Cup of Coffee" by Mel Tormé (1958)
- "Coffee, Tea or Me?" by Peggy Lee (1958)

A surreal image of a giant coffee mug suspended in mid-air, with people floating inside, each one engaged in a different activity - reading, writing, playing chess, or simply lounging. The image represents the diverse ways in which coffee has become an integral part of our daily lives, and how it can transport us to different worlds and realities.

Coffee as an ingredient in cooking, with a stack of coffee - infused desserts and pastries

Close - up of a professional barista
pouring latte art.

HOW COFFEE IS ENJOYED AROUND THE WORLD

A painting of a bustling street in Istanbul with small, independent coffee shops lined up on both sides, serving traditional Turkish coffee and other regional specialties

Coffee is a beloved beverage that has captured the hearts of people worldwide. From the bustling streets of New York to the quiet cafes of Paris, coffee is an essential part of daily life for millions of people. In every country, people have unique ways of enjoying coffee, with different traditions and customs surrounding this beloved drink.

In Italy, coffee is a way of life, and the espresso is king. Espresso is a strong, concentrated shot of coffee usually served in small cups, known as demitasses. The Italians enjoy their espresso standing at the bar, usually accompanied by a sweet pastry or biscuit. The art of making espresso is taken very seriously in Italy, and baristas are highly trained to produce the perfect shot of coffee with a thick crema on top.

In contrast, in Vietnam, coffee is traditionally enjoyed with sweetened condensed milk, creating a rich, creamy, sweet flavor profile. This unique take on coffee reflects the country's French colonial past and is typically served over ice, making it perfect for the hot and humid climate.

In Turkey, coffee has been an essential part of daily life for centuries. It is often enjoyed with a small glass of water and a sweet treat, such as Turkish delight or baklava. Turkish coffee is brewed using finely ground coffee beans and served unfiltered, creating a thick, sludgy texture.

The cultural significance of coffee is also fascinating.

In Ethiopia, the birthplace of coffee ceremonies are a daily ritual that brings families and communities together. The ceremony involves roasting and brewing coffee beans over an open fire and serving the coffee in small cups. It is a way of showing hospitality and respect to guests.

Coffee has long been associated with hospitality and generosity in the Middle East. Serving coffee to guests is a sign of respect and is often accompanied by sweet treats, such as dates or baklava.

In addition to its cultural significance, coffee has inspired art, literature, and music. From Vincent van Gogh's paintings to Ernest Hemingway's novels, coffee has served as a muse for many artists and writers. Coffee houses have also played an essential role in the intellectual and artistic movements throughout history, serving as a meeting place for writers, artists, and revolutionaries.

Coffee is more than just a beverage; it reflects culture, tradition, and community. Whether enjoyed in a bustling cafe in Paris or a quiet coffee house in Istanbul, coffee brings people together and inspires creativity and innovation.

An image of a latte art masterpiece, with intricate patterns and designs formed by the foam on top of the coffee

A person holding a steaming cup of coffee while sitting in a cozy café, with the warm glow of the interior lighting adding to the inviting atmosphere

COFFEE SHOPS AND THEIR ROLE IN COMMUNITIES

Oil painting of a cafe counter surrounded by people, in the style of dark white and dark bronze, soft, muted palette, Vancouver school, uhd image, industrial machinery aesthetics, fujifilm pro 400h, stock photo

Over the past few decades, coffee shops have become a cultural and social hub for many communities worldwide. They are more than just a place to grab a cup of coffee; they offer a cozy and inviting atmosphere where people can relax, socialize, and work. The popularity of coffee shops has led to a coffee culture that celebrates the art of coffee making and the enjoyment of coffee in all its forms.

Coffee shops are not only places to socialize and unwind, but they also play a significant role in the local economy. They create jobs and contribute to the growth of small businesses, supporting local farmers, roasters, and other coffee-related industries. In addition, coffee shops often serve as a platform for local artists, musicians, and writers to showcase their talents and contribute to the vibrant cultural scene of the community.

There are different types of coffee shops, from chain stores to independent cafes. Each one has the unique characteristics that make it stand out. Chain stores offer consistency and convenience with standardized menus and procedures, while independent cafes provide a more personalized and memorable experience focusing on specialty coffee and artisanal food. Many independent coffee shops pride themselves on their commitment to sustainability, sourcing their coffee beans from small farmers and using environmentally friendly practices in their operations.

Coffee shops are not just places to grab a cup of coffee; they reflect the community they serve. They provide a sense of belonging and offer a welcoming space for people of all backgrounds to come together and connect. Whether it's to catch up with friends, work on a project, or simply enjoy a quiet moment alone, coffee shops have become integral to modern life.

Adorable local coffee shop's collaboration with a local artist, showcasing artwork displayed on the walls and perhaps a small gallery event taking place, highlighting the coffee shop's role in supporting and promoting local artists and contributing to the cultural scene

Oil illustration of a bustling coffee shop interior, with people sitting at tables, enjoying their coffee and engaging in conversation, capturing the vibrant and social atmosphere of a local community gathering spot

COFFEE AND ART, LITERATURE, AND MUSIC

An oil painting of a coffee-themed music festival, with musicians performing on a stage surrounded by coffee vendors and enthusiasts enjoying the festivities

The relationship between coffee and the arts has a long and rich history, with coffeehouses serving as popular gathering places for artists, writers, and musicians throughout the centuries. From the bohemian cafes of Paris to the jazz clubs of New Orleans, coffeehouses have been integral to cultural movements and artistic communities.

Artists have found inspiration in the rich flavors and aromas of coffee and the lively atmosphere of coffeehouses. For example, the Dutch painter Vincent Van Gogh was known to be an avid coffee drinker, and some of his most famous works, such as "The Night Cafe," depict the bustling atmosphere of cafes. Similarly, the French impressionist Edgar Degas frequently painted scenes of cafes and their patrons, capturing the social dynamics of coffee culture.

Coffee has also played a significant role in literature, with many famous writers turning to the beverage for inspiration. For example, the American author Ernest Hemingway was known to be a heavy coffee drinker, and coffee features prominently in his novels, such as "The Sun Also Rises." Other writers, such as Honoré de Balzac and Voltaire, were known for their love of coffee and their role in their creative process.

In music, coffee has inspired countless songs, from the upbeat jazz standard "Black Coffee" to the more melancholic ballad "One More Cup of Coffee" by Bob Dylan. Coffee-themed music festivals have become increasingly popular in recent years, bringing together musicians and coffee enthusiasts worldwide.

One of the most exciting developments in the intersection of coffee and art is the rise of latte art. Baristas are now using steamed milk to create intricate designs on the surface of espresso drinks, turning each latte into a work of art. From simple hearts to elaborate portraits, latte art has become popular for baristas to showcase their creativity and add a personal touch to each drink.

The connection between coffee and the arts is a testament to the beverage's ability to inspire and unite people. Whether enjoyed in a quiet coffeehouse or a bustling cafe, coffee will continue to play a significant role in shaping culture and artistic expression.

Image reference + an artist in a coffeehouse, sitting with a sketchbook and a cup of coffee, engrossed in the creative process, surrounded by the lively atmosphere of the cafe.

Pencil sketch of a gallery exhibition dedicated to coffee-inspired artwork, showcasing paintings, sculptures, and other artistic expressions inspired by the flavors, aromas, and culture of coffee

HEALTH BEN-EFITS & CON-TROVERSIES

Coffee plays an important role in many people's lives and can have both positive and negative effects on health.

Coffee is a beverage that has been consumed for centuries, and its popularity continues to grow. While some people may drink coffee solely for its taste or to wake them up in the morning, others believe that coffee can significantly impact their health. Researchers have conducted numerous studies in recent years to explore the potential health benefits and risks of coffee consumption.

One of coffee consumption's most significant potential health benefits is its ability to reduce the risk of developing certain chronic diseases. For example, studies have found that regular coffee consumption may help reduce the risk of developing type 2 diabetes, liver disease, and some types of cancer. Additionally, coffee may positively affect heart health by reducing the risk of stroke and coronary heart disease.

On the other hand, some studies have suggested that excessive coffee consumption may negatively affect health. For example, high caffeine intake can cause restlessness, insomnia, and anxiety. Additionally, some people may experience digestive problems, such as acid reflux, after drinking coffee.

Despite the potential health risks associated with coffee consumption, many people continue to drink coffee daily. To maximize the potential health benefits of coffee, experts recommend consuming it in moderation and avoiding adding sugar or creamer. It is also important to note that everyone's body is different, and what works for one person may not work for another.

Overall, while the research on coffee's effects on health is still ongoing, it is clear that coffee is a beverage that is enjoyed by many people worldwide. By staying informed about the latest research and drinking coffee in moderation, people can continue enjoying this beloved beverage while promoting their health and well-being.

A coffee cup with a scale, representing the importance of moderation in coffee consumption for optimal health

Photo of a brunette drinking coffee in a serene and peaceful environment, promoting the idea that enjoying coffee can be a relaxing and enjoyable experience that contributes to overall well-being

Colored pencil drawing of a person enjoying a cup of coffee outdoors, with a backdrop of green fields and blue skies, symbolizing the connection between coffee and the beauty of nature, which can contribute to overall well-being

Acrylic painting of a close-up of a coffee bean surrounded by vibrant fruits and vegetables, emphasizing the potential health benefits of coffee, such as its antioxidant properties, which may contribute to overall health and disease prevention

THE HEALTH BENEFITS OF COFFEE

A person doing yoga while drinking coffee

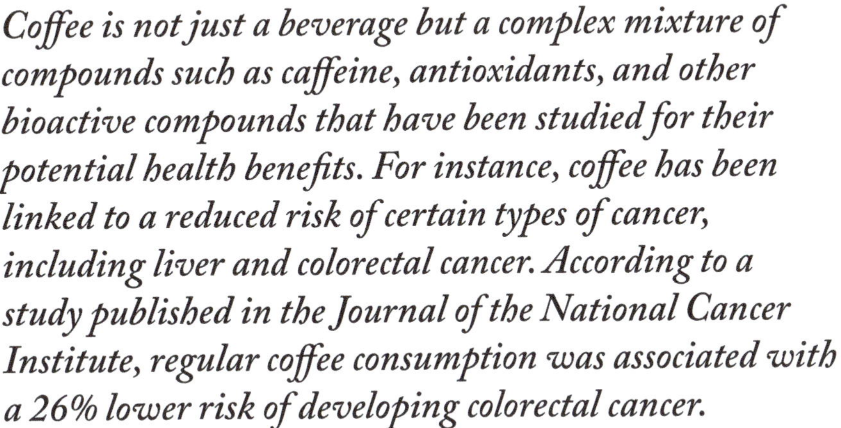

Coffee is not just a beverage but a complex mixture of compounds such as caffeine, antioxidants, and other bioactive compounds that have been studied for their potential health benefits. For instance, coffee has been linked to a reduced risk of certain types of cancer, including liver and colorectal cancer. According to a study published in the Journal of the National Cancer Institute, regular coffee consumption was associated with a 26% lower risk of developing colorectal cancer.

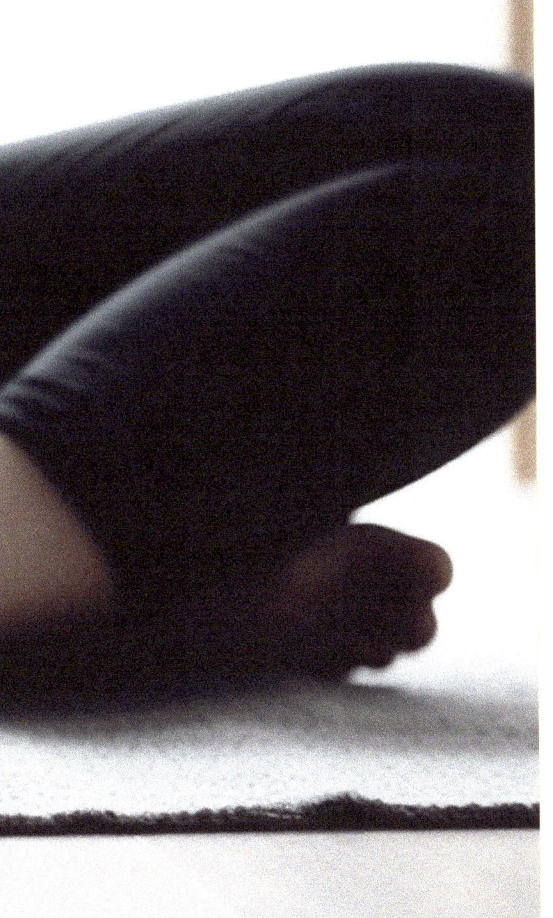

In addition to reducing cancer risk, coffee has also been shown to protect against neurological diseases. Several studies have found that coffee consumption reduces the risk of Alzheimer's and Parkinson's diseases. Moreover, caffeine, the primary ingredient in coffee, has improved cognitive function, attention, and alertness.

Research also suggests that coffee may have benefits for athletic performance. The caffeine in coffee has been shown to increase endurance and reduce perceived exertion during exercise. This is because caffeine stimulates the central nervous system, which can lead to increased adrenaline release and a subsequent boost in energy.

Moreover, coffee may also have mental health benefits. Studies have shown that regular coffee consumption is associated with a lower risk of depression and suicide. Researchers believe that the caffeine and other compounds in coffee may boost the production of feel-good neurotransmitters like dopamine and serotonin, which may help alleviate symptoms of depression.

While more research is needed to fully understand the potential health benefits of coffee, current evidence suggests that moderate coffee consumption may positively affect physical and mental health.

A coffee mug with a heart-shaped steam pattern rising from it, representing the potential cardiovascular benefits of coffee. The image suggests that moderate coffee consumption may contribute to heart health and overall well-being.

Charcoal drawing of a group of athletes drinking coffee before a workout or competition. The athletes are shown energized and ready to perform, representing the potential benefits of coffee on athletic performance and endurance

CONTROVERSIES SURROUNDING COFFEE CONSUMPTION

A person drinking a cup of coffee while exercising, representing the debate surrounding coffee's impact on athletic performance

Despite the growing body of research suggesting potential health benefits associated with coffee consumption, controversies surrounding its effects still exist. Some concerns have been raised about coffee's impact on cardiovascular health. While some studies suggest that coffee may increase the risk of high blood pressure and heart disease, others indicate that moderate coffee consumption may have a neutral or even protective effect on cardiovascular health.

Another area of controversy is coffee's potential to increase the risk of certain types of cancer, particularly bladder and pancreatic cancer. However, the research in this area is mixed, and some studies have even suggested that coffee consumption may reduce the risk of liver and colorectal cancer.

Coffee's impact on pregnancy and fertility is also a concern, as high levels of caffeine intake have been associated with an increased risk of miscarriage and preterm birth. However, moderate coffee consumption (less than 200-300 milligrams per day) is generally considered safe during pregnancy.

Caffeine, the main active ingredient in coffee, is also a source of controversy. While caffeine has been shown to have cognitive and performance-enhancing effects, it can also lead to anxiety, sleep disturbances, and addiction in some individuals. The amount of caffeine in a cup of coffee varies widely, depending on the brewing method and type of coffee beans used.

While coffee consumption has been linked to potential health benefits, it is important to consume it in moderation and be aware of potential risks or concerns.

Acrylic painting of a pregnant woman holding a cup of coffee, symbolizing the debate surrounding coffee's impact on pregnancy. The woman can be shown contemplating, conveying the need for moderation and awareness during pregnancy

Oil pastel drawing of a scale with coffee beans on one side and health-related symbols on the other, symbolizing the balance between the potential benefits and risks of coffee consumption

THE FUTURE OF COFFEE

The coffee industry is evolving at a dizzying pace

The future of coffee is a topic of great interest to many in the industry, as well as to consumers around the world. One major trend likely to continue is the emphasis on sustainability and social responsibility in coffee production. Consumers are increasingly concerned about the impact of their purchasing decisions on the environment and the communities where coffee is grown. As a result, many coffee companies are making a concerted effort to reduce their carbon footprint, implement fair labor practices, and support small-scale farmers.

Another area of innovation in the coffee industry is using technology to improve the quality and consistency of coffee. Advances in coffee roasting technology have led to the development of new techniques, such as infrared roasting, which allows for greater precision and control over the roasting process. Similarly, new brewing technologies, such as robotics in espresso machines, are helping to ensure that each cup of coffee is prepared with the same care and precision.

One trend likely to continue in the coming years is the growth of specialty coffee, which emphasizes high-quality beans and meticulous preparation techniques. This trend has led to the development of new brewing methods, such as the Japanese pour-over method, which requires a great deal of skill and attention to detail but can result in a cup of coffee that is both complex and nuanced.

Finally, climate change is likely to significantly impact the coffee industry in the coming years. As temperatures rise and weather patterns become more unpredictable, coffee farmers will face new challenges in growing and harvesting crops. This may lead to changes in the types of coffee grown and the regions where they are produced, as well as new innovations in farming techniques designed to adapt to a changing climate.

Overall, the future of coffee is bright, with exciting new developments in sustainability, technology, and quality. However, the industry will also face unique challenges as it adapts to a rapidly changing world, making it an exciting time to join the coffee community.

A coffee roasting machine with advanced technology that can monitor and adjust temperature and roasting time to achieve perfect consistency and flavor

An image of a coffee farmer using sustainable and environmentally friendly farming practices, such as composting and natural pest control, in a lush and vibrant coffee plantation.

A futuristic image of a coffee farm using advanced farming techniques to adapt to the challenges of climate change, such as hydroponics and vertical farming, in a landscape that reflects the changing weather patterns.

Crayon drawing of a coffee farmer using innovative farming techniques, such as vertical farming or shade-grown cultivation, to adapt to the challenges of climate change.

Crayon drawing of a coffee farmer using innovative farming techniques, such as vertical farming or shade-grown cultivation, to adapt to the challenges of climate change.

THE CHANGING LANDSCAPE OF THE COFFEE INDUSTRY

A futuristic image of a coffee farm using advanced farming techniques to adapt to the challenges of climate change, such as hydroponics and vertical farming, in a landscape that reflects the changing weather patterns

Climate change, economic instability, and changing consumer preferences are some of the biggest challenges the coffee industry faces in the 21st century. Climate change, in particular, poses a significant threat to coffee production as it affects the growth and quality of coffee beans. Rising temperatures, erratic weather patterns, and increased pest and disease pressure all threaten coffee yields and quality. This affects coffee farmers' livelihoods and the global coffee supply chain.

Economic instability is another challenge that impacts the coffee industry, particularly for small-scale coffee farmers. They often need more resources and infrastructure to compete with larger coffee producers, leading to lower prices for their coffee beans. This makes it difficult for them to sustain their businesses and support their families.

Consumer preferences have also shifted in recent years, with more people seeking high-quality, sustainably produced coffee. This has led to the rise of specialty coffee, which focuses on the unique flavor profiles of coffee beans and the way they are grown and processed. Direct trade involves farmers selling their coffee beans directly to roasters and retailers, which has become more prevalent recently. This allows farmers to receive fair prices for their coffee and enables consumers to learn more about the origin of their coffee beans.

The third wave of coffee is another emerging trend in the industry, characterized by a focus on quality and craftsmanship in coffee preparation. This trend has led to the rise of artisanal coffee shops and a renewed interest in traditional brewing methods such as pour-over and espresso.

As the coffee industry continues to evolve, it is crucial to address these challenges and find sustainable solutions to ensure its future success. This includes investing in climate-smart coffee production methods, supporting small-scale farmers, and promoting transparency and ethical practices throughout the coffee supply chain.

Blue pen drawing a coffee farm affected by climate change, showing wilted coffee plants and dry soil to represent the challenges faced by coffee growers due to rising temperatures and erratic weather patterns. The image can evoke a sense of urgency and highlight the need for climate-smart coffee productio

Watercolor of a coffee farmer and a roaster engaging in a transparent and fair transaction. The image can emphasize the direct connection between farmers and consumers, symbolizing the positive impact of direct trade on the livelihoods of coffee farmers and the quality of coffee beans

SUSTAINABILITY AND ETHICAL CONCERNS

A lush forest with coffee trees growing under a canopy of trees, representing shade-grown coffee and its positive impact on biodiversity.

Coffee is a commodity that significantly impacts the environment and the people who grow and harvest coffee beans. The coffee industry has been criticized for contributing to deforestation, soil degradation, water pollution, and greenhouse gas emissions. Moreover, many coffee farmers and workers are paid low wages and lack access to fundamental human rights.

Sustainable coffee is an approach to coffee production and consumption that seeks to minimize the coffee industry's negative environmental and social impacts. It involves a holistic approach to coffee farming that considers the health of the soil, water, and biodiversity and the well-being of farmers and workers.

One key aspect of sustainable coffee is shade-grown coffee. Shade-grown coffee is grown under a canopy of trees, which provides a habitat for wildlife, helps to conserve soil and water, and reduces the need for chemical fertilizers and pesticides. Shade-grown coffee also tends to have a richer flavor than sun-grown coffee.

Another aspect of sustainable coffee is fair trade. Fairtrade is a system that ensures that coffee farmers and workers receive a fair price for their coffee and are treated fairly and respectfully. Fair trade promotes social and economic development in coffee-producing communities by providing access to credit, education, and healthcare.

Consumers can support sustainable coffee by choosing coffee certified by organizations such as Rainforest Alliance, UTZ, and Fair Trade USA. These certifications indicate that the coffee has been produced in an environmentally and socially responsible way. Consumers can also buy coffee from local roasters and shops that source their coffee directly from small-scale farmers.

Coffee companies can also take steps to support sustainable coffee production. This includes investing in sustainable farming practices, supporting fair trade, and directly trading with small-scale farmers. Coffee companies can also reduce their environmental impact by using renewable energy, reducing waste, and minimizing their carbon footprint.

Sustainable coffee offers a way to enjoy coffee while supporting the health of the planet and the people who produce it. By choosing sustainable coffee and supporting ethical and sustainable practices, consumers and coffee companies alike can help to build a more sustainable and equitable coffee industry for generations to come.

Watercolor of a lush shade-grown coffee plantation, with coffee trees thriving under the canopy of tall trees. The image can showcase the natural beauty and biodiversity of shade-grown coffee farms, emphasizing the environmental benefits and the habitat provided for wildlife

Blue ink illustration of direct trade and supporting small-scale farmers, with a coffee company representative visiting a coffee farm and engaging in direct trade with the farmer. The image can convey a sense of partnership, transparency, and fair compensation, emphasizing the importance of establishing direct relationships between coffee companies and farmers to promote sustainability

THE FUTURE OF COFFEE TECHNOLOGY

Two image references + A coffee farmer and their family, representing the importance of fair trade and ensuring that coffee farmers and workers are paid fairly and have access to basic human rights

Innovation has always driven the coffee industry, and technological advances are rapidly changing how coffee is grown, harvested, processed, and consumed. In recent years, there has been a surge of interest in using technology to create more efficient and sustainable practices in the coffee industry.

One area where technology is making a significant impact is coffee harvesting and processing. Traditional methods of handpicking and processing coffee beans are time-consuming and labor-intensive and can lead to inconsistent quality. However, new technologies such as robotic coffee harvesters and automated processing equipment are helping farmers to streamline their operations and produce higher-quality coffee more efficiently.

In addition to coffee production innovations, technology is transforming how we brew and consume coffee. Innovative coffee makers and brewing systems use sensors and algorithms to precisely control water temperature, brewing time, and other variables, allowing coffee enthusiasts to create a perfect cup of coffee every time.

But technology isn't just improving the quality and consistency of coffee; it's also being used to help address some of the industry's most pressing challenges. For example, satellite imaging and precision agriculture tools are helping farmers to optimize their crop yields and reduce their use of water and pesticides, leading to more sustainable and environmentally-friendly farming practices.

The use of technology in the coffee industry is helping to create more efficient and sustainable practices while also improving the quality and consistency of coffee. As the industry continues to evolve, we can expect to see even more exciting innovations and advances in coffee technology in the years to come.

Gouache painting of a robotic coffee harvester in action, showcasing the use of technology in the coffee harvesting process. The robot is shown carefully picking coffee cherries from the trees, highlighting the efficiency and precision of automated harvesting methods

Sharpie drawing of an advanced coffee brewing system with sleek design and digital controls. The machine is shown brewing a cup of coffee, with water temperature and brewing time displayed on a screen, emphasizing the precision and control technology brings to the brewing process

SAVORING THE LAST DROP

Let's celebrate the enduring love for coffee and its continued significance.

Coffee is more than just a beverage - it's a cultural touchstone, a symbol of community, and a source of inspiration. From its ancient origins in Ethiopia to its status as a global commodity, coffee has played a vital role in human history and culture. In this book, we've explored the many facets of coffee, from its health benefits and controversies to its cultural significance and future potential.

As coffee lovers, we are responsible for appreciating the beauty and complexity of this incredible beverage while supporting sustainable and ethical practices that benefit coffee farmers, communities, and the planet. By learning more about the origins and history of coffee, the roasting and brewing process, and the changing landscape of the coffee industry, we can deepen our appreciation for this beloved drink and make informed choices as consumers.

We hope this book has inspired you to explore coffee's rich and diverse world and continue learning and growing as a coffee lover.

Despite the challenges and changes the coffee industry has faced, one thing remains constant: the enduring love for coffee. From the bustling cafes of Europe to the traditional coffee ceremonies of Ethiopia, coffee has a special place in the hearts and minds of people worldwide. Let's celebrate the enduring love for coffee and its continued significance.

We'll end with a call to action - to appreciate coffee's beauty and complexity, support sustainable and ethical practices in the coffee industry, and share our love for coffee with others. Whether you're a casual coffee drinker or a dedicated coffee enthusiast, we can all play a part in preserving and celebrating this beloved beverage for generations to come.

A heart shaped coffee cup has heart shaped hearts drawn in the top, in the style of digital airbrushing

Oil painting of an image of a community gathering around a pot of coffee, sharing stories and laughter

People from different backgrounds and cultures sharing a cup of coffee, highlighting the unifying and communal nature of coffee and its ability to bring people together across different languages, beliefs, and tradition

A person sitting in a cozy café, enjoying a cup of coffee while reading a book, surrounded by artwork and decor inspired by different coffee-growing regions, highlighting the role of coffee in art and culture

About the Author(s)

JERLYN X AI

A young woman is walking up steps next to building, in the style of life in new york city, english major, distressed materials, black arts movement, photo taken with provia, warmcore

Meet Jerlyn O'Donnell, Née Thomas, the Experience Designer behind this AI-generated coffee table book. Jerlyn has always dreamed of creating a book about coffee, and with the help of AI, she's made it a reality.

Jerlyn is a talented digital expert who creates captivating digital journeys that bring human purpose to life. With a keen focus on inclusiveness and accessibility, she expertly blends technology and art to reach a diverse audience. Her work has been featured on Vice.com, ESPN, and even Hillary Clinton's Instagram account.

But that's not all. Jerlyn is also an accomplished author, mentor, speaker, and published illustrator. She has run Ultramarathons and is a triathlete, completing a 70.3-mile race. When she's not busy pushing the limits of design, she's pushing her physical limitations.

Originally from Dominica, The Nature Island of the Caribbean, and raised in St. Croix, US Virgin Islands, Jerlyn now resides in the Bronx, New York, with her husband, Michael, and daughter, Mattis. To stay up-to-date with her latest projects and books, visit her website at commuteartist.com and follow her on Instagram at @commuteartist to see her beautiful artwork.

HOW THIS BOOK WAS CREATED

A lone black girl walking up some stairs, in the style of distressed materials, light indigo and dark green, paparazzi-style, everyday ephemera, stockphoto, cut/ripped

Using AI to create a book is an intriguing concept that has been in my mind for some time. However, I knew the right opportunity had to present itself before I could take on this challenge. As I continued experimenting with different AI tools, I noticed that the quality of the images produced by Midjourney version 5 had significantly improved. That was the moment when I knew it was time to take the plunge and create a book that AI entirely generated.

I turned to ChatGPT to write the content to ensure the book was completely AI-generated. I was amazed at how well the AI technology could create coherent, engaging sentences and paragraphs that flowed naturally. However, as with any creative endeavor, some challenges arose, such as ensuring correct grammar and punctuation. To refine the grammar, I used Grammarly, which helped ensure the writing was polished and professional.

Creating a book without human intervention can be daunting, so I included my prompts in the book. These prompts will inspire others to explore the use of AI in creative writing and to see what kind of unique and innovative ideas they can come up with. However, it's important to note that having an editor is critical to creating a successful book. I've always hired an editor in my other books, but I couldn't resist the urge to try this experiment on my own.

Finally, this book was a unique project that challenged me in ways I never thought possible. I'm excited to hear what readers think about it and receive feedback on this new and exciting way to create a book. This book will inspire others to explore the intersection of AI and creativity and think outside of the box regarding their own creative projects.

PLEASE NOTE: THE CONTENT IN THIS BOOK WAS NOT FACT-CHECKED.

"I'm excited to hear what readers think about it and receive feedback on this new and exciting way to create a book."

Men tending to the soil, in the style of digital painting, rural america, stephen shortridge, old timey, wet-on-wet blending, brushstroke fields, southern countryside -

Left Bottom: Image reference + men in a field, in the style of digital airbrushing, highly detailed, richly detailed genre paintings, depictions of labor, hdr, southern countryside, soggy

Top Right: Painting of men picking berries, in the style of hdr, soggy, digitally manipulated images, southern countryside, old timey, emotive fields of color, earthworks

Bottom Right: White men are working in an agricultural field, in the style of realistic with impressionistic colors, victorian-inspired illustrations, wet-on-wet blending, frogcore, melting pots, photo-realistic techniques, southern countryside

Did you know? The first webcam was created to monitor a coffee pot at the University of Cambridge, allowing researchers to check if the coffee pot was full or empty without leaving their desks.

Coffee is the second most traded commodity in the world, surpassed only by crude oil. Here's some other fun facts:

1. Coffee is a popular beverage prepared from the roasted seeds (coffee beans) of the Coffea plant.
2. The earliest evidence of coffee consumption dates back to the 15th century in the highlands of Ethiopia.
3. Coffee cultivation and trade expanded from Ethiopia to the Arabian Peninsula and eventually spread worldwide.
4. The two primary species of coffee plants used for commercial production are Coffea arabica and Coffea canephora (Robusta).
5. Brazil is the largest producer of coffee, followed by Vietnam, Colombia, and Indonesia.
6. The cultivation of coffee typically occurs in regions located between the Tropics of Cancer and Capricorn, known as the "Coffee Belt."
7. The coffee production process involves planting, harvesting, processing (removal of the pulp, fermentation, and drying), roasting, grinding, and brewing.
8. Various brewing methods are used to prepare coffee, including espresso, drip brewing, French press, and Turkish coffee.
9. Coffee beans contain caffeine, a natural stimulant that can enhance alertness and reduce fatigue.
10. The caffeine content in a cup of coffee can vary depending on factors such as the type of bean, brewing method, and serving size.
11. Coffee has been the subject of scientific research, with studies indicating potential health benefits, including reducing the risk of certain diseases such as type 2 diabetes and Parkinson's disease.
12. However, excessive coffee consumption can have negative effects, such as sleep disturbances, anxiety, and gastrointestinal issues.
13. The coffee industry faces environmental challenges, including deforestation, water usage, and the use of pesticides and fertilizers.
14. Fair trade initiatives aim to support coffee farmers by ensuring they receive fair prices for their products and promoting sustainable farming practices.
15. Coffee has a significant cultural impact, with coffeehouses and cafes serving as social hubs for gatherings, intellectual discussions, and artistic inspiration throughout history.

1. Pendergrast, M. (2010). Uncommon Grounds: The History of Coffee and How It Transformed Our World. Basic Books.
2. Clark, J. (2018). The ultimate guide to coffee. Penguin.
3. Ricci, M. (2017). The World Atlas of Coffee: From Beans to Brewing - Coffees Explored, Explained and Enjoyed. Mitchell Beazley.
4. Thompson, R. (2018). Coffee: A Global History. Reaktion Books.
5. Pergola, P., & Marcone, M. F. (2018). Coffee and its consumption: Benefits and risks. Critical Reviews in Food Science and Nutrition, 58(16), 2676-2687.
6. Whitehead, A. (2019). Coffeehouses: The emergence of a social institution in 17th-century England. Routledge.
7. Williams, K. E. (2019). Coffee Culture: Local Experiences, Global Connections. Routledge.

An oil painting of a close-up image of a barista pouring espresso from a beautiful vintage espresso machine into a small cup

SOURCES& DISCLAIMER

While this book is a unique experiment in using AI to generate written content and images, it's important to note that it should not be taken as a definitive source of information. The content and images generated by AI are based on algorithms and patterns, which means that they may only sometimes be wholly accurate or reliable.

Therefore, readers must do their due diligence and fact-check any information the book presents. This is especially important when it comes to critical or sensitive topics. It's always a good idea to verify information from multiple sources and consult with experts in the field to ensure the information is accurate.

That being said, this book is intended as an experiment in creativity and innovation. It's a coffee table book meant to be enjoyed for its unique content and AI-generated images. It's a fun and exciting way to explore the intersection of AI and creativity and see what unique ideas and creations can come from using AI technology.

So while readers should approach the content of this book with a critical eye, I hope they will also appreciate it for what it is: a fun and innovative experiment in using AI to generate written content and images.

www.ingramcontent.com/pod-product-compliance
Ingram Content Group UK Ltd.
Pitfield, Milton Keynes, MK11 3LW, UK
UKHW060020300726
14090UKWH00020B/1083